101 WAYS TO
JUMP-START
YOUR
INTUITION

101 Ways to Jump-Start Your Intuition

John Holland

HAY HOUSE, INC.

Carlsbad, California • New York City
London • Sydney • Johannesburg
Vancouver • Hong Kong • New Delhi

Published and distributed in the United States by: Hay House, Inc.: www.hayhouse.com • *Published and distributed in Australia by:* Hay House Australia Pty. Ltd.: www.hayhouse.com.au • *Published and distributed in the United Kingdom by:* Hay House UK, Ltd.: www.hayhouse.co.uk • *Published and distributed in the Republic of South Africa by:* Hay House SA (Pty), Ltd.: www.hayhouse.co.za • *Distributed in Canada by:* Raincoast: www.raincoast.com • *Published in India by:* Hay House Publishers India: www.hayhouse.co.in

John Holland's editor: Simon Steel • *Editorial supervision:* Jill Kramer
Design: Summer McStravick & Tricia Breidenthal

Library of Congress Control No.: 2004115022

ISBN 13: 978-1-4019-0619-1
ISBN 10: 1-4019-0619-2

14 13 12 11   11 10 9 8
1st printing, June 2005
8th printing, December 2011

Printed in Canada

"*Intuition is a reminder of the power of the human spirit.*"
— John Holland

CONTENTS

Introduction 1

101 Ways to Jump-Start
    Your Intuition 3

The Energy of Colors Chart 209

Energy Centers 211

About the Author 213

INTRODUCTION

Intuition is the language of the soul. We're all born aware with a profound sense of inner knowing. It's one of the greatest gifts we possess, which keeps us connected to our higher selves, the universe, and to our divine spirit. At one time or another, we will all experience flashes of intuition, especially when it's vying for our attention. It's those hunches, or gentle nudges, that we so often ignore or try to wave off as being simply our imagination — only to find out later that they were correct.

I've written this book to show you the many ways in which you can develop, access, and above all, *trust* your intuition. I've created 101 different ways to do so that will enable you to tap in to this vital resource — one that is deep within all of us and that can be harnessed and trained. All you need is a little help to *jump-start* it, so you can use it in every area of your life.

These 101 lessons are fun, quick, and easy to learn. You can read one lesson every day, or simply open the book and know that whatever lesson you choose is the one that was meant just for you. All the lessons include an affirmation or positive statement that will serve as a tool to help you harness your inner guidance.

In some of the lessons, I offer instructions on the energy centers of the body, how the physical body acts as a receiver for intuitive information, and how color affects us individually — all of which contributes to the flow of intuitive energy and how we all receive information differently. I've also included a color guide in the back of the book and a chart containing the location of the energy centers to help you benefit from the appropriate lesson.

Since so many people enjoyed my first two books, *Born Knowing* and *Psychic Navigator,* I've also included a few thoughts from each to assist in these teachings. Developing your intuitive abilities only takes a commitment to yourself, a dedication to understanding and learning how to live in partnership with your inner guidance. Enjoy each of the lessons, and have fun as you discover and develop your intuition. After all, it's an unlimited resource for guidance, transformation, and self-empowerment, which you can use and share for the rest of your life.

101 Ways to Jump-Start Your Intuition

*I trust my
intuition
and myself*

We're *all* equipped with a complex and highly tuned inner-guidance system, which we can access and use anytime we wish. Receiving intuitive information is all about *energy*, and people, places, and objects are all comprised of it. Since you too are energy, you can receive and read information via your intuitive senses. So trust . . . and give yourself permission to explore, play, and develop your intuitive ability so that you can see yourself — and the world — in a way you never thought possible!

IMAGINATION

*Imagination is
the playground
of intuition*

A well-developed imagination is a healthy part of your intuition. Have fun with your imagination as you expand your intuitive senses. Take a moment and imagine the perfect career, partner, home, or whatever you wish. Use all your senses! What does that feel like? Let the energy of excitement run through you. You'll begin to feel yourself smiling. Imagination is a powerful tool that could lead you to the bridge that connects you with your intuition, and the manifestation of what you truly desire.

*I acknowledge
and act upon my
body's messages*

*Y*ou already possess the most fundamental piece of intuitive equipment. You need look no further than your own physical body for answers. The next time you're making a decision, just pause for a moment, breathe deeply, and focus on your body. Begin to notice how it's trying to talk to you. It could be a gut response, a tingle up your spine, a hunch, or an emotion. Embrace what you're feeling as your body works in partnership with your intuition.

I give myself permission to visit my sacred space as often as I wish

*E*veryone needs their own special place — a place to think, reflect, meditate, and be alone with themselves and with Spirit. So, try to find a space that you can call your own. Feel free to create an altar with your favorite adornments, incense, candles, or even photos of spiritual figures that inspire you. By creating your own special area and using it for your quiet time, meditation, and personal development, you'll find that the entire area becomes infused with positive energy as it acquires its own special feeling.

*I choose to make
a commitment to
myself — and my inner
guidance — at this time*

$\mathcal{I}$ntuitive information can show up anytime or anywhere, so it's a good idea to create your *own* Intuition Journal. You may want to keep several journals in different places so that no matter where you are, there will be somewhere to record those intuitive flashes, impressions, or even your dreams. Your journal will be a valuable resource for you in the future to monitor your progress. By making an effort to write in your journal, you're making a commitment to your intuition, your spirit, and yourself.

My intuition works with me and for me

Psychic ability is the natural extension of intuition. Practice using your intuition and it will create a stronger link with your psychic awareness. Be free, and have fun working in this way. Ask yourself, "How many e-mails will I receive this morning?" When the phone rings, see if you can guess who's calling. You can make up many more ways to practice on your own. Initially, don't worry if you're right or wrong, for you'll begin to stretch and tap in to your psychic potential.

I am a beautiful expression of life

We're all uniquely different and possess our own individual intuitive strengths. Always remember that you'll develop in your own way, in your own time. Don't rush. Some people are feelers, whereas others will be more visual, and some of you will listen to that small, still voice inside. When you work with your ability, begin to notice if you're feeling, seeing, or hearing the information. By doing so, you'll strengthen that individual faculty, and eventually, all your strengths will begin to work collectively.

*I safely receive
and feel only what
is best for me, as
well as others*

We all have an inner sense of knowing. It's that gut feeling. Have you ever met people and have instantly known if you were going to like them or not? Have you had a gut feeling that you didn't follow, only for it to be proven correct? Next time you're about to make a decision, stop for a moment and ask yourself, "How do I feel about this decision? Does it feel positive or negative, and why?" By following your intuition, you'll be guided to make better choices.

*Intuitive vision lets you
see more of what is
really in front of you*

*S*ome people have the intuitive ability known as clear seeing (or *clairvoyance*). It's when intuitive information forms pictures, symbols, words, and colors in your mind's eye. The reception area is right between your eyebrows. To develop this ability, simply place a candle safely in front of you, relax, take some deep breaths, and gaze at the flame for a few minutes. Close your eyes and observe the afterimage. Let it fade, and do the exercise again to strengthen your third-eye area.

23

*I now notice
when my
inner voice is
speaking to me*

*D*o you know what others are thinking? Do songs suddenly come to mind at times? This is known as inner hearing. It can be confusing when determining if these are *your* thoughts or intuitive information. When you're outdoors, stretch your hearing by listening to sounds far off in the distance, then listen to the sounds that are closer to you. As you hear all the sounds together, listen inwardly *between* the sounds. This is where the intuitive information flows and can be heard.

11 FINDING THE STILLNESS

Every day in every way, I take time to find the stillness within me

*S*ometimes answers aren't always found on the outside, but can be discovered within. Intuitive guidance can be yours when you learn to still the mind. How do you silence that mind chatter? Meditation. Try different meditation techniques. Practice for at least 15 minutes a day, just for one week. You'll quickly notice your conscious thoughts becoming quieter, and intuitive guidance will start to flow. Also, by meditating regularly, you'll find that all areas of your life will benefit. Enjoy the stillness.

MAKING POSITIVE CHOICES

I now choose to bring positive energy into my day, as well as my life

It's always your choice as to what kind of day you want to have. Every day brings new opportunities, with purpose and new beginnings. Do something positive for yourself today — whether it's a walk, an afternoon nap, or a talk with a good friend. Take some time especially for yourself. You deserve it! Intuition flows even more freely when infused with positive energy. Live this day to the fullest — after all, you gave up a day of your life for it.

TRAINING THE MIND

Every day in every way, I expand my intuitive abilities

A great game I used to play with my mother was "Pick a number." I had no idea that I was training my young psychic mind. Here's how to play: Ask a friend to think of a number from 1 to 50 and see if you can visualize it. Go with the first answer that pops into your mind. Don't do it too many times because you'll begin to guess instead of intuit. These exercises may seem elementary, but what's happening is that you're beginning to stretch your abilities.

Breath is life;
life is the breath

Intuition flows on the breath. It's also filled with the universal energy that enhances your overall well-being. Close your eyes and just breathe deeply. Let the breath be the vehicle that carries you inward toward calmness and your inner guidance. Slowly let the breath come in and go out again, easily and effortlessly. Bring the awareness of the breath into your life today, and spend some time not doing anything! Focus on just being in the now.

HELPING THROUGH VISUALIZATION

The good in me can help the good in others

Intuition and psychic energy have no limits and can help everyone. If there's a person or a pet in your life in need of assistance or healing — you can help! Lie down and breathe deeply. Close your eyes and imagine a beautiful white light in front of you. Breathe in this white light and let it surround you. Imagine in your mind's eye whom you want to help. Visualize them happy and whole as you send them this divine light, which now surrounds them with healing energy.

I now attract all that I need in my life that is for my highest good

*E*veryone and everything is surrounded by an *aura* of magnetic energy. Auras hold the energy of what we attract to ourselves. All thoughts, emotions, and feelings are contained in the aura and are sent out to the universe. Quite simply, *what we think, we'll attract*. If you're afraid, you'll attract fear; if you're kind, you'll attract kindness; when you're grateful, you'll attract prosperity. Remember: You'll attract exactly what you're resonating. Ask yourself occasionally, "How are my thoughts today?"

I am beginning to be aware of the vibrations that surround everyone and everything

The aura, which extends beyond your physical body, is a sensitive detection system. Notice when you approach a place or a situation that doesn't feel right. Similarly, at social gatherings, be aware of those times when you find yourself drawn to a certain person or when you feel the need to distance yourself from someone. In these instances, stop and take note of how you're feeling, what you're sensing, and even what colors you perceive. By doing so, you're letting your inner guidance give you some intuitive insight that may be useful.

*My body is
my temple*

Honor and take care of your body so that your health becomes a top priority when you're developing your intuition. Your body acts like one huge psychic antenna, operating at its own level of receptivity. Spiritual philosophies teach us that the universal life force runs through everything, including *you*. Make sure that you get plenty of rest, eat properly, and go out in nature, as this will promote a healthy body and remove the blocks that prevent intuition from flowing freely.

41

*Every living
thing is a
rainbow
of colors*

Colors are a wonderful tool to lead you to your intuition. Let your imagination help you think in color. Close your eyes and picture someone you know. What color or hue do you imagine around them? When meeting new people or a situation arises, ask yourself, "What color are they or the situation emanating?" Go with the first color that comes to your mind. As you learn what colors mean, you'll never look at them in the same way again!

*My body is a
sensitive piece
of psychic
equipment*

*Y*our energy centers are the conduits in which universal energy and intuitive information flow. These precious centers run up and along your spine, so when you're working with your intuition, it's always best to make sure that you check your posture — whether you're standing or sitting comfortably in a chair. Keep your posture in check, as this will assist you in removing blockages and imbalances in your energy centers. By doing so, intuitive information has a better chance of getting your attention. Notice how you're standing or sitting right now!

I am strong, balanced, and here in the now

*T*he *root center* is related to our earthly issues, such as survival, our physical body, money worries, personal safety, and shelter. Dancing, physical exercise, walking, tai chi, or yoga will assist you in balancing this base center as well as ground you. The color red is associated with this center. Notice all the different hues of red today, and absorb them into your system. Honoring your body, and taking care of it on the *outside*, will benefit you on the *inside*. It works both ways!

*The passion
of life flows
through me
continually*

The sacral center relates to our emotions, desires, creativity, and sexuality. When this center is balanced, we live life with passion and excitement. The vibrant color orange is associated with this center. Focus on the many hues of orange today. Imagine that it surrounds you and pulsates through your sacral center. Practicing yoga, moving your hips, expressing your sexuality, and nurturing yourself will assist in balancing this center. Let the passion of life dance and flow through you as you move toward what you truly desire.

INTUITIVE INFORMATION

Intuition is the language of the soul

As you begin to work with your intuition, you'll start to notice how you're recognizing and differentiating intuitive information from your own thoughts. Record these moments in your journal as you feel an unexpected thought or impression come to mind. Draw pictures or symbols that are imprinted upon you. Write down affirmations that work for you, as well as your personal goals and desires. This will lead to a gradual awakening of how you interpret the language of your soul.

Everything is possible, and I can achieve anything

The *solar-plexus center* represents power, vitality, sensitivity, self-esteem, and confidence. This is a strong center where feelings, emotions, and intuitive signals are received. When this center is balanced, you'll resonate confidence and begin to trust yourself and your intuition even more. The bright color yellow is associated with this center. Imagine that there's a shimmering golden light resonating from your stomach area. Let it assist you in becoming all that you are, but even more important, all that you can be!

25 LOVE AND COMPASSION

I am love

The heart center represents unconditional love, compassion, joy, balance, relationships, and healing. It's said to be the link between our mind, body, and spirit. Forgiveness, self-love, and acts of compassion will assist in healing and balancing this center, as well as your spirit. The restorative color green is associated with this center. Notice all the healing hues of green around you, and breathe them into your heart area. Give your heart center what it needs today. You're worth it.

*I express myself
clearly, and I
do matter*

The *throat center* represents communication, expression, sound, and creativity. We have a habit of *not* speaking up, which can cause blockages. Humming, singing aloud (the shower is a great place for this), and chanting can assist in balancing this center, and the soothing color blue resonates with it. Imagine a beautiful blue sky before you, breathe in this color, and let it surround you and move through this center. Ask yourself, "Do I need to speak up or say something that needs to be said?" Express yourself!

The soul never speaks without a picture

*T*he *third-eye center* represents inspiration, imagination, intuitive perception, and guidance. With this center balanced, it's easier for your intuition to place symbols, pictures, or words in your mind's eye, and you'll be able to visualize solutions that aren't necessarily apparent. Strengthen this center with meditation techniques using visualization, color, or breathwork. The color associated with this center is indigo. Imagine this color between your brows, and see yourself happy and successful as you continue to connect with your spirit and your inner guidance.

The universe flows through me and continually guides me

The *crown center* is your link with the universe; infinite, divine wisdom; and your higher consciousness. Meditation balances this center with inner peace and calmness, and helps build awareness of your connection with everyone and everything. Violet is the color associated with this center. Imagine that pure violet light is flowing into this center from above, washing over you like a fountain. As you strengthen this center, you'll develop an *inner knowing* of what is true for yourself as well as others.

SEEING WHAT YOU FEEL

*Everyone
and everything
is made up
of energy*

*P*sychometry means "measure of the soul."

It's the practice of holding someone's personal possession and then reading the object. It's as if you're sensing or seeing through your hands. Ask a friend for an object that belongs to someone else. Close your eyes and give off the information that's coming into your mind *before* your logical mind kicks in. What are you feeling? Are there any pictures, letters, words, or colors? Okay, now try holding someone's business card — and see what you feel!

*Positive energy
flows through
and around me
at all times*

When you're taking a shower, imagine that the refreshing water is infused with healing white light. Stand under the water, place and keep your left hand on the bottom of your lower back, and then put your right hand in front of you over each energy center in turn. Now, work with all the centers one by one. You'll become more aware of your energy centers just by placing a cleansing thought on each one. Give it a try . . . and enjoy this spiritual wash!

65

MAKING DECISIONS

*I trust that the decisions
I make will enhance
all areas of my life*

*I*ntuition can be an excellent resource in assisting you with making decisions or choices. Try this technique: Imagine two roads in front of you with individual signs representing each decision. Take your time as you walk down each road, and observe all the surroundings. Notice everything. Do you feel positive or negative? Are the roads rugged or smooth? Is the landscape rich with greenery, or is it barren? Use this technique prior to making a small decision at first, then do more as you build your confidence.

I am energy

Our intuitive energy is a precious resource that can help us in most situations. The next time you can't find something in your house, try this exercise: Close your eyes and imagine that energy is expanding all around you. Let it seek out what you're looking for. Let it move through your entire home. Notice if an image or word comes to mind. Is a particular room being shown to you? Go to that part of your home and see if you're correct.

FOLLOWING THE INTUITIVE BREATH

As I breathe, awareness follows

Close your eyes and take a deep breath. Relax, and let your awareness bring you back into your body. Follow your breath to the quiet place within your heart. Take a few breaths into this area and continue to relax and feel grounded. Your body and mind will begin to grow quieter with each breath. Next, bring your awareness into your solar-plexus area, and ask your intuition if there's something it wants to tell you. Breathe, and pause here for a moment, acknowledging whatever comes.

71

*The subconscious
constantly speaks
through our dreams*

Dreams are an excellent way for our intuitive mind to speak to us, so creating a Dream Journal is a good way to start this process. Before you go to sleep tonight, ask your intuition a specific question that you need answered. As soon as you awaken and *before* your feet touch the floor, write down what stood out in the dream — the people, places, and more important, the emotion in the dream. Try to interpret what your dream is telling you, and look for intuitive symbols and answers to your question.

*As I develop
my intuition, I
become more
receptive*

*Y*ou can train yourself to be intuitive and have fun at the same time. Get a deck of playing cards and shuffle them. Without looking, place four cards face down. Now rub your hands briskly together and take one hand, palm down, and let it float above the four cards. Which are red or black? You might get a warm sensation for red and a cold one for black. Go with the first feeling you receive for each card. It sounds simple, but the more you practice, the better you'll get.

The more I give, the more I receive

Here's a great way to start your day! Stand outdoors or near an open window. Spread your arms open wide, and take a deep breath. As you inhale slowly and deeply, feel the universal force entering your whole body, right into every nerve cell and fiber of your being. Hold this breath for a moment. Then as you slowly exhale, send your blessing to the world and everyone in it. We are and always will be connected to each other.

CONNECTING WITH YOUR FEELINGS

Intuition and feelings are the best of friends

*S*o many people often approach me for intuitive information and ask, "What do you think about this?" or "What do you think about that?" Sometimes I say, "Well, I'm not sure what I think about it, but . . . this is what I'm *feeling*." The next time you have a decision to make, check in with your feelings first — *before* you proceed. Ask yourself, "How do I feel about this?" and "Why do I feel this way?" Trust yourself. Connect with your feelings and your intuition.

*The gift of
awareness lies in
the discovery of
your intuition*

he next time you're feeling a mental block or need some intuitive guidance, get a book or magazine and place it firmly in the palm of your hands. Think of the question and quickly open the book and point without looking to any words. Observe where your finger lands. You may discover that the word or sentence spurs new ideas, images, or feelings that will assist you in thinking outside the box. Hopefully this will help you with what you're seeking.

A BEING
OF LIGHT

*Imagine yourself as
a being of energy
and light — because
in reality, you are*

Your aura plays a vital role alongside your intuition. Intuitive information flows through the aura when it's expanded, charged, and energized, so you might try this exercise: Make yourself comfortable, sitting or lying down with your back straight. Close your eyes, relax, and breathe deeply. Imagine that you're a tube of light. This radiant light enters from below you as well as above you. Let it energize and expand your aura as it flows completely through you. Let it remove all blockages so that intuitive information can be received freely and clearly.

83

A wealth of information is available to me anytime I wish

*I*n our digital society, we've all grown accustomed to having information at our fingertips. Here's a great way to use visualization and your imagination to download intuitive answers. Find a comfortable chair and sit up straight. Close your eyes and visualize a giant computer screen in front of you. Type in a question and hit the "Enter" key. See your question on the "screen." Wait a moment — you may receive back a word, or even a sentence. Record what you receive.

*I focus my
attitude on
gratitude*

Gratitude encourages intuition and abundance. Be thankful for who and what is in your life — instead of complaining about what you don't have. Appreciate all the abundance and goodness that's around you, whether big or small. Be thankful for your health, children, sunny days, your garden, family, best friends, or even the person who let you jump ahead in line at the bank. The more joy you begin to notice and appreciate, the easier it is for your intuition to lead you to even more happiness and prosperity.

HIGHER AWARENESS

Awareness is simply a higher knowing

We're all connected to divine awareness, although we have a tendency to pull away from this source. When you need help with a question or require some direction, let your higher mind help you out. Take a breath, close your eyes, and imagine that a bright white light is coming up through your body and out the top of your head. As the white light sits above your head, put the question inside the light. See if you get a clear answer to your question. Remember — think up!

43 MANIFESTING

I know what I want and where I'm going

How do you make your goals and desires come alive? Having a clear picture in your mind (of the *highest good*) and charging it with energy can help turn it into reality. Visualize a goal in its final resolution. Now *feel* what it's like to have a successful outcome. See it happening here and now. Maintain and charge this image as you breathe energy into it. Feel the excitement, the energy, and the joy. Let it go, trust, and release it to the universe.

Knowledge takes time, but from it comes wisdom

*T*he more knowledge you have in your mind, the more your intuition has to work with. Subscribe to information-packed magazines such as *National Geographic, Time*, or *Scientific American* — anything that will expand your mind and your consciousness. Let the pictures and stories move you and inspire your thoughts. The mind is far more than a mere storage library — it's a finely tuned creative instrument that will assist you in shaping your reality and your future.

45

RECEIVING GUIDANCE

Intuition is waiting for you to simply ask for its guidance

Imagine any decision or choice in front of you, such as: "Should I proceed with this project?" or "Is this person right for the job?" Now ask, "How do I feel about this decision?" and "How will I feel about it a year from now?" Notice how your body feels. Is it light? Heavy? Tense? Are you sensing colors, symbols, or words? Write them down without thinking, *before* your mind tries to rationalize them. Congratulate yourself! You just received information from an intuitive perspective.

46

STRENGTHENING YOUR AURA

As I strengthen my aura, only positive energy can enter my space, and only positive energy can go out

When your *aura* is strong and healthy, it acts as a protective shield to help you stay emotionally and mentally strong and physically healthy, and also enhances your intuitive abilities. To strengthen your aura, maintain a balanced and healthy diet; try to get outdoors more often; breathe in clean, fresh air; exercise regularly; and go for a massage or bodywork. Take time to rest, relax, and meditate regularly. All of this will greatly assist in building your intuitive strength as you reinforce your precious aura.

97

47

UNDERSTANDING OTHERS

*I am able to
share and trust
my true feelings*

When you sense or feel a negative mood emanating from someone, try this useful technique to understand what's going on with them — before you blame yourself. First, get *yourself* out of your own way. Discard the thoughts relating to what you're perceiving or feeling. Relax, close your eyes, and breathe. Try to imagine that you're stepping into their shoes and becoming that person. Feel what they're feeling. See if you now have a better understanding of what's *really* happening and how you could possibly help.

*Using and
trusting
intuition leads
to clarity*

Intuition is received via your feelings, energy centers, and emotions. One of the best ways to improve your receptivity of intuitive impressions is to stop watching television (at least for a while). We've let TV do our thinking and imagining for us, so our own intuitive senses have become lazy. Try reading the newspaper more or tape the shows you feel you really can't miss. By doing so, your own *inner screen* will develop in strength and become more receptive, and clarity will soon follow.

STRETCHING YOUR INTUITIVE ABILITIES

*I safely receive
information
for myself
and others*

*A*sk a friend to tell you the name of someone *they* know but you don't. Imagine a rose in your third-eye area (any color you wish) and concentrate on this name. Notice if the rose is opening, blooming, or slowly closing. Is it wilting, or is it simply just bending? Let your own intuitive awareness interpret the clues from the rose, and tell your friend what you're perceiving and feeling. This is a great exercise to help you build and stretch your intuitive abilities.

Breath is power

The human body is sustained by the same *prana* (energy) that nourishes the universe. With normal breathing, we inhale and exhale a regular amount of prana. When depleted of prana, we often complain about feeling tired or unwell. Go to the mountains, a forest, or anywhere where there's greenery. Breathe in slowly and deeply to a steady rhythm. By controlling and regulating your breathing, it's possible to absorb more of this valuable and vital energy source.

Your loved ones are just a thought away

*L*ove is the energy source that connects us to each other. If you haven't heard from a family member or friend in a while, try this experiment: Close your eyes and picture that person. See everything about this individual — hear their voice and feel their personality. Send them a thought to contact you. Over the coming days, don't be surprised when they call and say, "I've been thinking about you," or "I felt like I just wanted to call and say hello." We're all connected.

52

RHYTHMIC BREATHING

Breathing to a rhythm is like dancing with the universe

*F*ind a comfortable place to lie down. Rest your hands lightly over your stomach area. Breathe slowly and steadily to a calm rhythm. With each breath, create a mental picture of energy rushing in through your nostrils and flowing right down into your lungs. Imagine this energy as sparkling white light as it's being absorbed in your solar plexus. Now visualize this energy being distributed throughout your body — in every bone, muscle, and nerve ending. Let it strengthen your body, mind, and spirit.

53

TOTAL RELAXATION

Taking the time to relax is my right — my gift to myself and my spirit

Relaxing the body will assist you in stilling your mind and tapping into your intuition. Find a peaceful place to sit, and take a slow breath. Close your eyes and imagine a brilliant white light entering your feet from the ground. Let the light travel up your calves, your legs, your back, your head, down your shoulders, your arms, and out through your fingers. Let the light relax every part of your body. Use this technique anytime you're feeling tense or stressed.

*Vibrations are
the heartbeats
of my intuition*

Everything is made of energy, which constantly moves and vibrates. Even colors have their unique vibration and frequency. Have someone sit across from you and ask this person to *think* and *feel* a color. Tell him or her to imagine the color surrounding their entire being. Now place your hands, palms out in front of you, toward that person. Notice if you're feeling, seeing, or even hearing a particular color. The more you experiment, the more you'll know how you're receiving the information. Have fun!

The magnetic energy that surrounds me has no limits

Do you sometimes feel cut off from people, places, or even society? We all have the capacity to feel everyone and everything. Remember, you're a magnetic being with an aura that can expand and contract at will. Go for a walk outdoors and imagine that your aura is extending beyond your physical body. Let it blend and become one with everything around you. There are no limits. Don't forget to pull back your aura when you're finished. Always know that you are a part of all that is.

*Life shows
me miracles
every day*

*W*ith so much information in this world vying for your attention, intuition can be easily missed. Synchronicities and coincidences are clear signs that intuition is knocking on your door. Have you heard the same phrase or saying from more than one person today? Do the same numbers keep showing up in your life? Has someone mentioned the same person you were just thinking of? These are all just signs for you to pause, be open, and pay attention. There are no accidents in this intelligent universe.

I now attract all the right people into my life

People come into your life for a reason. Some you learn from and they move on, whereas others return because you need to learn more from them. Others stay with you throughout your entire life. Take a good look around you, and ask yourself, "Are there people in my life who are supporting and encouraging my spirit to learn and grow?" Find a support group or an awareness class to share your spiritual experiences, and in turn, others will be learning from you as well.

The more I trust and let go, the more I am guided

*D*iscovering who we are and what we want are constant endeavors for most of us. Know that your intuition wants to help guide you and be your partner in discovering what you truly desire and need. Sometimes you have to let go of the riverbank to see where life wants to take you. Be courageous, take challenges, be willing to trust, and learn to let go so that your inner guidance can lead you to new discoveries and exciting opportunities. Go with the flow!

121

I have the ability to write my own future

*T*rusting and following your intuition is like writing your own life story. Every day is like turning a page, a new beginning. Close your eyes, take a deep breath, and imagine how you'd like to see yourself. Envision your life 5, 10, and 20 years from now. Try to *see* and *feel* yourself in a life you truly desire. Let your intuition help lead you on your path, and remember that it's not just the destination, but the journey along the way that's the most interesting!

60

FINDING YOUR PASSION

When you have passion, intuition has no boundaries

Passion is a clear sign that your intuition is working and you're following its guidance. You'll notice a feeling of excitement and enthusiasm flowing through you when you're doing something you truly love. So many people say to me, "I don't know what I'm passionate about." Try to remember when you were a child and what you were passionate about then. Seek out what makes you excited. If that passion can help you and be shared by others, then it's all worth it.

61

POSITIVE THOUGHTS

Life follows thought

Try to think positively today and repel any negative thoughts. Try not to judge yourself or others . . . which may be harder than you imagine. However, by doing so, you'll change your reality, because thoughts are made up of positive and negative energy, and this directly affects your life. When you think a thought, your aura will magnify it with energy and put it out to the universe. By monitoring your thoughts, you'll have conscious control in shaping your future.

*I live in the
powerful
present
moment*

A walking meditation is a beneficial alternative when sitting meditations are getting too repetitive. With each step, begin to count from one to ten. Then count from ten down to one, and start again from one up to ten. As you walk and count, keep your focus on the sole of each foot as it hits the ground. What's happening as you count one, two, three, four, and so on to your steps is that you're bringing your awareness and focus back to the powerful present.

*Everyone and
everything is
connected, and
always will be*

*W*hen you have the opportunity on a clear night, go outside and look up at the night sky and the heaven of stars. Take in a deep cleansing breath and just be there in the moment. This helps to expand your consciousness. Try to see the vastness and wonder of the universe, to know that you are one with it all. The same energy that makes up the universe . . . is in you.

*I release all fears
and doubts;
I am free*

Is it time to let something go? Time to release it to the universe and know and trust that it will be taken care of? You have to make room for energy, intuitive guidance, and abundance to flow through you. Ask yourself, "What's in my life that I no longer need?" By releasing and letting go, you're opening yourself up to your own higher consciousness, and by doing so, you're making room for more of what's for your highest good.

I enjoy opening,
and working with,
my intuition

*H*ave fun while you strengthen your intuition. One way to do so is to try this short exercise with a friend: Stand upright with both hands behind your back, with both palms up. Then have your friend put sugar in one hand and salt in the other, without telling you which is which. See if you can discern which is the salt and which is the sugar. By doing so, you're using your body as a piece of sensory equipment. Some people can *intuitively* taste the difference!

Everything in the Universe has a spark of awareness

All animals are living, feeling, and sensitive beings. They don't need words to know what you're feeling, as they can intuit your emotions. You can have better communication with your pet by simply using your intuition. Try this experiment: Get yourself comfortable, clear your mind, and call out lovingly to your pet in your mind. Do this a few times and see if your pet responds. Once you begin to practice intuitive communication with animals, a whole new relationship will begin.

137

*My intuition
works with me
and for me*

Playing with your intuition, along with your imagination, can only make it stronger. The next time you're watching an athletic event or movie, try to guess intuitively what the final score will be, or how the movie ends. You don't need to tell anyone, and you don't have to do it *all* the time (it's okay to just enjoy the event!). This is just another great way of stretching your intuitive muscles.

LISTENING WITH YOUR INTUITION

Intuitive energy continually flows through the spoken word

The voice is a powerful medium for picking up intuitive information. The next time you're on the phone with someone, close your eyes and really listen to the voice on the other end. Let the person's tone and words completely enter your space so that your intuition takes over from your conscious reaction. You may notice colors, images, or even feelings that have nothing to do with the conversation. So, don't just listen with your ears; listen with your intuition.

*As I send out
loving calmness,
all those around
me are affected*

Colors are powerful tools to inspire and motivate, as they can often instill a sense of calmness and peace in you. The next time you encounter someone who's irritable, whether it's a co-worker, a tired waiter, or even a crying child, try this technique: In your mind, send them a soft shade of pink. Imagine that they're totally surrounded in this tranquil color, and watch how their mood changes for the better and they appear to calm down. Try it and just "think pink"!

143

See it — believe it — become it

*W*e all have the ability to influence and guide our own destiny. Imagine an event, such as an interview that's coming up in the near future. Try using your imagination to *see yourself* at that interview. Take a good look around and notice anything and everything. Is your intuition providing you with valuable information that could create a more positive outcome? Write down everything you feel and perceive. In this case, foresight can be a wonderful thing. So next time, *look* before you leap.

145

When we leave this world, all we take with us is what we did or did not do

*J*ust for today, make your main purpose serving and giving back, without expecting anything in return. Reach out and touch other people's spirit. It's quite likely that someone out there really needs it today. The kindness you give will reinforce that person's belief and faith that there are people who really care. One act of kindness can create a ripple effect. Maybe you'll make this daily act of giving a part of your life forever. Share and spread the energy.

*Intuition
is always
readily
available;
I just
need to
step back
and ask*

*T*here are three positive words that can help you anytime you're feeling stressed or disconnected from your intuition. They are: "Find your center." When you say or think these three words, it immediately draws you back to your inner self. You'll find yourself back at that place of calmness where your intuition has a clearer channel to communicate with you. Try repeating these words frequently throughout the day and you'll remain in check with yourself as well as your spirit.

73

ACHIEVING CLARITY

Tapping into your intuition is like taking in a deep cleansing breath of clarity

Because we live in a fast-paced world, we rarely make time for ourselves. Meditating for just one minute can greatly help your overall well-being and act as the catalyst to jump-start your intuition. Take a moment during the day to close your eyes. Breathe deeply and relax for a minute. By doing so, you'll feel calmer, centered, and more focused. This will leave you with a renewed sense of clarity that stays with you throughout the day. Enjoy this minute — just for you.

151

74

THE PRESENT MOMENT

*I am here —
in the present,
in the moment*

Part of noticing intuitive signs, signals, and those gentle nudges is becoming more conscious of what you're doing in your everyday life. If you're having a cup of tea, then just drink your tea. If you're enjoying a meal, then just eat your meal. If you're walking, just walk. Appreciate, focus, and be in the moment. By doing so, you'll remain in the powerful present, and that way, your intuition has a better chance of getting your attention.

153

By giving my intuition free reign, the possibilities are endless

Grab your journal. On the top of the page, write down a question you'd like some intuitive guidance on. Now keep the question in your mind as well as in front of you. Place your pen on the page and start writing whatever comes to you. Don't think! Let yourself go as you write, make shapes, or just doodle. Do this for a few minutes without stopping. You're giving your intuition free reign to go where it wants, before your logical mind gets in the way.

76

SUNRISE BLESSINGS

I add joy to my life, and I am living my life to the fullest

Something magical and wondrous happens when the sun rises to bless us with a new day. But most of us sleep right through it. You can be closer to your spirit at this special time. Occasionally, get up early and watch the sun come up, write in your journal, meditate, and just feel the energy that's all around you. The deep feeling of peace and connection to your spirit at this early hour will remain with you throughout your entire day.

77

USING YOUR CREATIVE SIDE

Intuition floats on the edge of creativity

As children, we lived our lives using the more creative "right" side of our brain. As we got older, we had a tendency to pull away from our right side and rely more on the intellectual "left" side of our brain. So try doing something creative, such as taking a class where you can sketch, draw, write, paint, color, sing, or do whatever works for you. Wake up your spirit as you get back in the flow of using your creative and intuitive side once again.

78

RESTING YOUR BODY

My body is my ultimate teacher. I honor and respect it

*A*s you develop your intuitive abilities, it's perfectly okay to take a break for few days or however long you need — don't push it. Imagine how your radio sounds when the battery is low and the reception weakens. So it is with your physical body. You are *here* in the physical world, so stay balanced and grounded with your physical life as well as your spiritual life. Rest, relax, nurture yourself, take an aromatherapy bath, or go to bed earlier. You deserve it.

*True intuitive
answers arise
from the silence
within ourselves*

When others start telling us their problems, too many of us respond instantly with what we believe would be best. Quick responses or quick fixes are *not* always the best way, since that person may only be venting or expressing their thoughts. Sometimes we must recognize when it's right to be silent. Use your intuition wisely. By letting others' issues and problems soak into your own consciousness and your intuition, you can offer a more considered response — if one is really needed.

163

A PROTECTIVE AURA

The spiritual light of protection flows through me and surrounds me at all times

*A*s you develop your intuition and strengthen your inner guidance, it can have the effect of enhancing your sensitivity to everyone and everything. Notice how some people or places make you feel energized, while others leave you feeling drained. Learn to strengthen your aura with protection. As you get dressed each morning — just *before* you start your day — remember to place a protective thought on your aura. See your aura as a brilliant white light that acts as an invisible shield, surrounding you throughout the day.

The energy of life flows through me and inspires me at all times

We all have the capacity to connect with our spirit and divine guidance. So, too, we've experienced those feelings of being cut off, uninspired, and often disconnected from life at some time or another. Learn to open up your crown energy center again to bring the intuitive connection back. Sit up straight, and imagine a healing white light entering through the top of your head, as it moves and circulates down through your entire body. Your body, mind, and spirit will be restored and unified again.

167

USING INNER GUIDANCE

*Intuition equals
possibilities*

*B*y using your intuition continually, you can improve its strength so that you develop a keen sense of when it's trying to communicate with you. Persistence and dedication are necessary, but you can have a lot of fun along the way! There are plenty of opportunities to practice using your inner guidance. For example: "Which elevator door will open next? Which checkout line will move faster? Who's on my answering machine?" Think of other ways to practice, because, as you know . . . practice makes perfect!

The one thing that really stops most of us from succeeding is not believing in ourselves

*T*he power of intuition really has no boundaries when it comes to its many uses. Try this exercise to improve and expand the range of your abilities: Have a friend cut out three completely different photos from a magazine and place them in separate envelopes, so you can't see them. Place the three envelopes in front of you and let your intuition *reach* inside the envelopes and see what colors, images, shapes, or patterns you sense. Take your time and write down your impressions.

*All numbers have
their own frequency
and speak to us in
their own language*

When numerology and intuition work together, you can truly observe how the magic of numbers affects us. Calendars, birth dates, the seasons, and the rotation of the planets all reflect a numerical sequence of order. Numerology is a fun, easy system to learn and can provide a structure that can help you understand the different cycles in your life, and enhance awareness, both in yourself and others. Once you become hooked on numbers, you'll never look at them in the same way again!

The Universe has a rhythm — if people would simply stop and listen

OM is one of the universal words, and is the primal sound that emanates from the entire universe. By continually chanting this sacred sound during a meditation, it will revitalize your energy centers; harmonize your mind, body, and soul; and instill peace and inner calmness. It will also raise your vibration to a higher consciousness, and in doing so, clear the channel for intuition. OM is a word of power. Try chanting it slowly ten times during your next meditation. Enjoy the vibration!

Focus and concentration are keys to intuition's door

To improve your intuitive abilities, you also have to learn to focus on the extraordinary power of your mind. Intuitive information can be frequently downloaded into your consciousness, and could be fleeting. By learning to concentrate intently, you'll be able to hold on to the information longer. Try this exercise: Grab a pencil, rock, flower, or anything you wish; and study everything about it: the size, texture, color, and shape. Although this is a simple task, it does benefit your intuition, focus, and concentration immensely.

I now notice everything around me . . . as well as in me

Before you begin to enhance your intuition, I often suggest that you look around your own physical world first. Notice all that's around you: the color of the sky, the green grass, the different people on the street — all the colors and variations you can see. Of course, everything you see isn't always pleasant or beautiful, but try to acknowledge whatever you can. Your intuition is a natural extension of your *human* senses, so by stimulating them, you'll enhance your *inner* senses.

*My intuition
allows me
to blend and
connect with
everyone and
everything*

*N*ature is a wonderful conduit for energy to assist you in developing your intuition. Try this exercise: Ask a friend to bring you a flower that someone else held for at least ten minutes. Take the flower and gently hold it by the stem, letting your intuition take over as you assimilate and give off any information you're receiving. Don't analyze, don't critique — just receive. It's as if holding this beautiful flower is opening the door into another world.

89

MOVEMENT AND CHANGE

Life and intuitive information move to a continual universal dance

Everything in life is in a process of movement and change. It's how the universe works. Intuition also flows and moves, but often we unconsciously hinder the flow and seem to be stuck without answers. Let's get the flow going again! Ask a question of your intuition, and put on some music that you usually don't listen to. Let yourself dance and move to the music. Your intuition now has more freedom to experiment, and the space to dance in order to give you intuitive guidance.

90

RECOGNITION AND KNOWLEDGE

By recognizing the divine in others, I am acknowledging the divine in myself

When you meet people for the first time, you might find that images and feelings just pour into your mind. It can be such a strong feeling that you instantly form a picture of them, or you have a sense of what their profession is. Similarly, you may pick up on people and conditions that are around them. What's really going on is that you're actually reading and interpreting someone's *aura*. Recognize and know that there's so much more around you than just what you can see.

91 MOVING FORWARD

Dwelling on the past diminishes the power of the future

Too many of us have regrets about things we've done, or we often catch ourselves saying "could've," "would've," or "should've." Worrying about what we already did — or didn't do — doesn't bring back anything. Don't be that *"If only I had . . ."* person. It's far better to acknowledge and accept it all and move on to something else. Learn the lessons that you were meant to learn, and let your intuition guide you to move forward to a positive future — one with no regrets.

*We receive
exactly what
we expect
to receive*

Before you start your day, take a few minutes for yourself. Relax, close your eyes, and breathe. Begin the day by asking a question of your intuition in your mind. Imagine that it's going out on a loudspeaker to the universe. Know and expect that an answer will come to you. Don't just sit back and wait for it — look to see if your intuition has put someone or something in your path that has your answer. Remember, intuition can arrive in many forms.

My intuitive abilities are getting stronger every day

*I*ntuition can be activated in many ways. Here's a fun exercise to try: Have a friend show you a few signatures of people whom you don't know. Run your fingers over the signatures and trace their names. It doesn't matter how their penmanship is, for what you're doing is tapping into the personalities and lives of these people. Are they calm, excited, negative, or positive? See if you can pick up anything else. Don't be surprised if you truly amaze yourself!

My intuition can be developed by joining with others

You don't always have to develop your intuition by yourself. Invite a few friends over to participate in this exercise: Place a bowl of water on a table. While you're out of the room, have one of your friends place their hands around the bowl for a few minutes. The energy of that person is now on the bowl and in the water. Look into the water through your third-eye center. Who held the bowl? What else can you perceive? Experiment and have fun!

*I remember to
pause and ask
before I act*

In today's busy world, we have a tendency to plow through important decisions without consulting our intuitive inner guidance. Then we kick ourselves later, saying, "Why didn't I think it through?" or "What made me do that?" Here's a tip to help you pause and ask *before* you rush into making a hasty decision: Find a small crystal and place it on your desk as a reminder to check in with your intuition. Another tip is to try taping an intuitive affirmation onto your computer.

My breath and I are one

Mindfulness is the opposite of distraction. It's the ability to maintain an easy sense of focus and attention — to keep your mind from shifting from thought to thought. The answer is in the simple act of *mindful breathing*. The more mindful you are, the more you're aware of yourself and what's going on inside of you, as well as what's going on outside and beyond yourself. Study the *mindfulness* of breathing, and it could change your life!

THE PULSE OF LIFE

I am a beautiful expression of life

*T*he pulse of life runs through everything, and your intuitive vibe rides on this current. People feel the pulse of life in numerous ways. Some of us feel it while exercising; some hear it in music, and others notice life as they walk in a big city. Yet life doesn't always come to you — you must seek it out. Notice where and when you feel the current of life's energy. When you *feel* the energy, know that intuition is usually not far behind.

*I chant in order
to jump-start
my intuitive
batteries*

*H*ave you ever noticed how people chant different tones as they're sitting in meditation? It's an ancient tradition of charging up and vibrating their energy system. Each of the seven main energy centers has its own unique frequency and vibration. Using sound with them can be a powerfully energizing and invigorating experience. Experiment with the ritual act of "chanting," as it might be exactly what you need to jump-start those all-too-often dormant intuitive batteries.

Every day my abilities become more enhanced

*A*s children, we're quite psychically aware. As we grow up, our rational minds are easily influenced by our parents, teachers, and the power of the media. Consequently, the intuitive right side of our brain gets used less and less, as the left (more analytical) side starts to take over. Remember, everyone develops their intuition in their own way and in their own time. It's not a race. Have patience with yourself — after all, it's like learning an exciting new language all over again.

100 BEING RESPONSIBLE

I appropriately act on my intuition

You must be responsible when using your intuitive abilities. The most important thing is to proceed slowly and stay balanced. Keep in mind that you have to honor *all* of you — physically, emotionally, mentally, and spiritually. You're exploring a whole new path that should never be forced upon anyone else — it's your path. When the time is right, friends and colleagues may begin to question things outside themselves, and you can be there for them. As they do, they'll also look inward to find their *own* answers.

*I open the doors
to the wonder
and discovery
of my spirit*

*T*o live an intuitive life, you must *believe* and *know* that you're equipped with all the tools you need. As a spiritual being, you possess unlimited abilities, so it would be wise to recognize the potential that's waiting to be awakened. As you meditate, try to focus on yourself as a spiritual being. The same energy that's in life, God, the universe, and nature is inside you — your spirit. Believe in your spirit and intuitive abilities. They've always been there . . . and always will be.

207

The Energy of Colors

RED: Vitality, passion, temper, energy, strength

ORANGE: Creativity, joy, sensuality, emotions, warmth

YELLOW: Intuition, sensitivity, intellect, happiness, fun

GREEN: Love, healing, compassion, earth, balance

BLUE: Spiritual, peace, communication, imagination

INDIGO: Perception, inner awareness, knowledge, freedom

VIOLET: Wisdom, beauty, inspiration, creativity, enlightenment

WHITE: Truth, innocence, purity, energy

BROWN: Grounding, earth, nature, calm

GOLD: Spiritual, inspiring, leadership, wisdom

Energy Centers

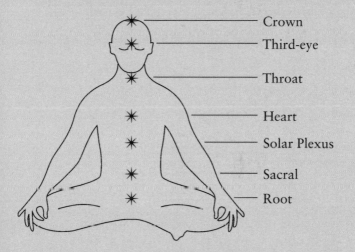

- Crown
- Third-eye
- Throat
- Heart
- Solar Plexus
- Sacral
- Root

ABOUT THE AUTHOR

John Holland, the best-selling author of *Born Knowing* and *Psychic Navigator*, is an internationally renowned psychic medium who has been lecturing, demonstrating, and reading for private clients for more than 15 years. He's dedicated to his ongoing personal development, which inspires him to continue teaching others about the incredible resource called "intuition" that's readily available to everyone.

John's *FREE* (e-mailed) newsletter includes tips on developing your psychic and intuitive abilities, interviews with other authors, book reviews, and helpful Website links.

To contact John by mail and/or to sign up for his free e-mail newsletter:

John Holland
P.O. Box 983
Exeter, NH 03833
www.JohnHolland.com

We hope you enjoyed this Hay House book. If you'd like to
receive our online catalog featuring additional information on
Hay House books and products, or if you'd like to find
out more about the Hay Foundation, please contact:

Hay House, Inc.
P.O. Box 5100
Carlsbad, CA 92018-5100

(760) 431-7695 or (800) 654-5126
(760) 431-6948 (fax) or (800) 650-5115 (fax)
www.hayhouse.com® • www.hayfoundation.org

✳

Published and distributed in Australia by:
Hay House Australia Pty. Ltd., 18/36 Ralph St., Alexandria NSW 2015
Phone: 612-9669-4299 • Fax: 612-9669-4144 • www.hayhouse.com.au

Published and distributed in the United Kingdom by:
Hay House UK, Ltd., 292B Kensal Rd., London W10 5BE • *Phone: 44-20-8962-1230*
Fax: 44-20-8962-1239 • www.hayhouse.co.uk

Published and distributed in the Republic of South Africa by:
Hay House SA (Pty), Ltd., P.O. Box 990, Witkoppen 2068
Phone/Fax: 27-11-467-8904 • info@hayhouse.co.za • www.hayhouse.co.za

Published in India by: Hay House Publishers India, Muskaan Complex,
Plot No. 3, B-2, Vasant Kunj, New Delhi 110 070 • *Phone: 91-11-4176-1620*
Fax: 91-11-4176-1630 • www.hayhouse.co.in

Distributed in Canada by: Raincoast, 9050 Shaughnessy St.,
Vancouver, B.C. V6P 6E5 • *Phone: (604) 323-7100*
Fax: (604) 323-2600 • www.raincoast.com

*

Take Your Soul on a Vacation